Planets in Our Solar System

NEPTUNE

by Steve Foxe

PEBBLE
a capstone imprint

Pebble Explore is published by Pebble, an imprint of Capstone.
1710 Roe Crest Drive, North Mankato, Minnesota 56003
www.capstonepub.com

**Library of Congress Cataloging-in-Publication Data is available on the
Library of Congress website.**
ISBN 978-1-9771-2398-5 (hardcover)
ISBN 978-1-9771-2698-6 (paperback)
ISBN 978-1-9771-2435-7 (eBook PDF)

Summary: Far off Neptune holds many mysteries! Its great distance from
the sun makes it the coldest planet in the solar system. Discover the secrets
of this chilly, blue ice giant that was named after the sea.

Image Credits
NASA: JPL/USGS, 20, 26; Science Source: Chris Butler, 22, Julian Baum,
24, MARK GARLICK, 17, NASA, 10; Shutterstock: alexaldo, 6–7, Artsiom
Petrushenka, 27, ChameleonsEye, 28, Dotted Yeti, Cover left, Back Cover,
1, 21, eurobanks, 19, NASA images, Cover, Nostalgia for Infinity, 25, Oleg
Golovnev, 16, oorka, 5, SkyPics Studio, 12, Vadim Sadovski, 8, 11, 13,
YummyBuum, 9; Wikimedia: ESA/Hubble, NASA, L. Calçada, 23, NASA on
The Commons, 15

Design Elements
Shutterstock: Arcady, BLACKDAY, ebes, LynxVector, phipatbig, Stefan
Holm, veronchick_84

Editorial Credits
Editor: Kristen Mohn; Designer: Jennifer Bergstrom; Media Researcher:
Tracy Cummins; Production Specialist: Tori Abraham

All internet sites appearing in back matter were available and accurate
when this book was sent to press.

Table of Contents

Words in **bold** are in the glossary.

Neptune, the Last Planet

Neptune is far, far from Earth. It is the eighth **planet** in the **solar system**. It is the farthest planet from the sun.

The eight planets move in a circle around the sun. Their paths are called **orbits**. It takes Earth one year to circle the sun. It takes Neptune 165 years! This is because Neptune is so far from the sun.

Mercury Earth Uranus

Venus Mars Jupiter Saturn **Neptune**

Neptune is the eighth planet from the sun.

Jupiter

Saturn

Planets in size order from biggest to smallest

Planets spin while they circle the sun. One full spin is one day. Neptune circles the sun slowly. But it spins very quickly. A day on Earth is 24 hours. A day on Neptune is about 16 hours.

Uranus   Neptune   Earth   Venus   Mars   Mercury

Neptune is much larger than Earth.
More than 57 Earths could fit inside
Neptune! But weight on the planets is
nearly the same. You would weigh just
a little more on Neptune than on Earth.

Pluto

Our solar system used to have nine planets. Pluto was the ninth. In 2006, **scientists** decided Pluto was a **dwarf planet**. A dwarf planet is smaller than a planet.

Neptune is closer to the sun than Pluto is. But sometimes their paths cross. Then Pluto is closer to the sun than Neptune is. The last time this happened was in 1979. It will happen again in 2227.

Neptune's orbit crosses with Pluto's.

Pluto

Neptune

The Bright Blue Ice Giant

The planets Neptune and Uranus are called **ice giants**. The ice on these planets is not like ice on Earth. Ice on Neptune is frozen **gas**. Neptune has no ground to stand on. The planet may have oceans under its ice.

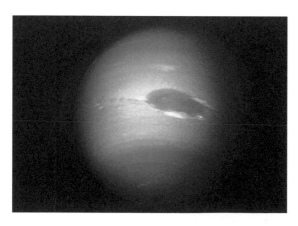

Frozen gases on Neptune

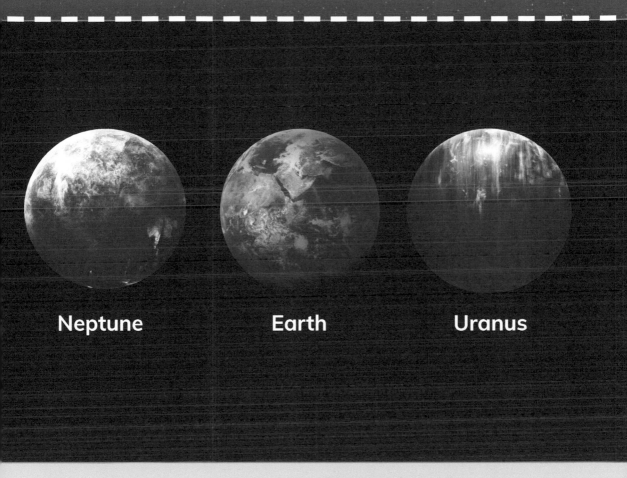

Neptune　　　Earth　　　Uranus

Three blue planets

Neptune and Uranus are both blue planets. A gas around them scatters blue light. Earth is also blue. Earth's oceans make it look blue.

Neptune's core

Neptune is very cold. It gets very
little heat from the sun. But the
planet has a hot **core** inside. Neptune
makes more heat than it gets from
the sun.

Sunlight travels very fast. But Neptune is far from the sun. It takes sunlight more than four hours to reach Neptune. It takes sunlight about eight minutes to reach Earth. Sunlight is not bright on Neptune.

Neptune gets little sunlight.

Neptune's Windy Weather

Neptune has four seasons. Each season lasts about 40 years! Every season is very cold.

Strong winds blow around the planet. Neptune's hot core might be why. Heat from the core mixes with the cold gases. That makes wind.

The winds on Neptune can turn into large storms. One storm was called the Great Dark Spot. This storm was as large as Earth! It lasted about five years.

Great Dark Spot

The Math Planet

Long ago, people did not know about Neptune. It is the only planet that cannot be seen with the eye alone. Scientist Galileo saw Neptune in 1613. He used a **telescope**.

Galileo sharing his telescope

He thought it was a star, not a planet.

In 1846, people were studying Uranus. They measured its path using math. Something was odd. There seemed to be another planet after Uranus. They searched with telescopes. They found an eighth planet. It was Neptune!

Uranus

More than one person helped find Neptune. They did not agree about who found it first. People are still not sure.

The planet was almost named after a French man. People outside of France did not want that. So Neptune was named after the Roman god of the sea. This is a good name for a cold, blue planet!

Statue of the Roman god Neptune

Triton, the Backward Moon

Neptune has at least 14 moons. Its largest moon is Triton. It is larger than Pluto.

Triton circles Neptune the opposite way of the planet's spin. It is the only large moon in the solar system that does this.

Triton

Neptune and some of its moons

Triton may have been a dwarf planet
before. A dwarf planet circles the sun.
A moon circles a planet. Neptune may
have pulled Triton in to make it a moon.

Triton is one of the coldest spots in the solar system. It is covered in ice. It also shoots ice miles above the planet!

Art showing Triton's ice geysers

Hippocamp
is the name of
Neptune's newest moon.

Neptune's other moons were
found more than 100 years after
Triton. The other moons are small.
Neptune's newest moon was found
in 2013.

Long Trip to Neptune

NASA launched a **probe** in 1977. It flew past Jupiter and Saturn.

The probe went to Uranus and Neptune next. It got to Neptune in 1989. It is the only spacecraft to visit the planet.

Art of Voyager 2 near Triton

Neptune's rings

The probe took many pictures. It found six new moons. It also saw that Neptune has rings. Before that, people were not sure if the planet had rings. Neptune's rings are much smaller than the planet Saturn's large rings.

The probe showed us Neptune's large storms. It also took photos of Neptune's long, white clouds. These clouds stretch across the planet. Now big telescopes watch Neptune's weather.

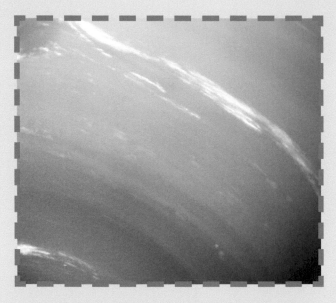

Neptune's white clouds

Telescope in space

A new probe would take more than 12 years to reach Neptune. There are no plans yet to send another probe to the planet.

Neptune is the last planet in the solar system. It is not easy to study up close. There is still so much to learn about it. Maybe one day you will help find out more about faraway Neptune!

NASA station in Australia

Fast Facts

Name:
Neptune

Location:
8th planet from the sun

Planet Type:
ice giant

Discovered:
Galileo saw it with his telescope in 1613. He thought it was a star. In 1846, two astronomers discovered that Neptune was a planet.

Moons:
14

Glossary

core (KOR)—the inner part of a planet or a dwarf planet that is made of metal or rock

dwarf planet (DWAHRF PLA-nuht)—a large object in space that orbits the sun but is not large enough to be a planet

gas (GASS)—something that is not solid or liquid and does not have a definite shape

ice giant (EYESS JIE-uhnt)—a planet made up mostly of ice and liquids

NASA (NA-suh)—National Aeronautics and Space Administration, which runs the U.S. space program

orbit (OR-bit)—the path an object follows while circling an object in space

planet (PLAN-it)—a large object that moves around a star

probe (PROHB)—a small vehicle used to explore objects in space

scientist (SYE-un-tist)—a person who studies the world around us

solar system (SOH-lur SISS-tuhm)—the sun and the objects that move around it

telescope (TEL-uh-skohp)—a tool people use to look at objects in space

Read More

Adamson, Thomas K. *The Secrets of Neptune*. North Mankato, MN: Capstone, 2015.

Baines, Becky. *Planets*. Washington, D.C.: National Geographic Kids, 2016.

Sommer, Nathan. *Neptune*. Minneapolis: Bellwether Media, 2019.

Internet Sites

All About Neptune
https://spaceplace.nasa.gov/all-about-neptune/en/

Neptune: The Windiest Planet
https://solarsystem.nasa.gov/planets/neptune/overview/

Facts About Neptune
https://www.scienceforkidsclub.com/neptune.html

Index